JOSEPH CONRAD

To Mary and John Reilly

JOSEPH CONRAD

Jim Reilly

Life and Works

Jane Austen
The Brontës
Joseph Conrad
Charles Dickens
T. S. Eliot
Thomas Hardy
Hemingway
D.H. Lawrence
Katherine Mansfield
George Orwell
Shakespeare
John Steinbeck
H.G. Wells
Virginia Woolf

Cover illustration by David Armitage

First published in 1990 by
Wayland (Publishers) Ltd
61 Western Road, Hove,
East Sussex BN3 1JD, England

© Copyright 1990 Wayland (Publishers) Ltd

Series adviser: Dr Cornelia Cook
Series designer: David Armitage
Editor: Susannah Foreman

British Library Cataloguing in Publication Data
Reilly, Jim
    Joseph Conrad. – (Life and works)
    1. Fiction in English. Conrad, Joseph, 1857–1924 –
    Critical studies
    I. Title II. Series
    823'.912

    ISBN 1–85210–811–8

Typeset by Rachel Gibbs, Wayland
Printed in Italy by G.Canale & C.S.p.A., Turin
Bound in the UK by Maclehose & Partners, Portsmouth

Contents

1

Conrad's Careers

Joseph Conrad was a man of many and striking contradictions. The novelist John Galsworthy said of him that he had never met a man who was so masculinely keen and yet so femininely sensitive. The novelist and critic Virginia Woolf wrote that Conrad lead a 'double life', and that in order to imagine all those 'fundamentally simple and heroic . . . gnarled and tested' sea-captain characters whose virtues he praises, 'one must be possessed of the double vision':

> To praise their silence one must possess a voice, to appreciate their endurance one must be sensitive to fatigue. One must be able to live on equal terms with the Whalleys and the Singletons and yet hide from their suspicious eyes the very qualities which enable one to understand them. Conrad alone was able to live that double life, for Conrad was a compound of two men; together with the sea-captain dwelt that subtle, refined analyst whom he called Marlow. 'A most discreet, understanding man', he said of Marlow.

Woolf's image of Conrad as 'a compound of two men' echoes the theme of one of the most psychologically revealing of all his stories, 'The Secret Sharer'. Originally to be called 'The Other Self' or 'The Secret Self', it tells how a sea captain, whom the reader senses is Conrad himself, secretly harbours an escaped seaman who has killed a fellow crewman. These two characters can be said to represent different aspects of Conrad's personality. The

Opposite *Joseph Conrad in 1923.*

captain stands for the traditional discipline of the merchant service to which Conrad was devoted, and the fugitive stands for the rebellious outcast often explored in Conrad's writings. The two characters experience a strange closeness as if they were not two characters, but one. The captain feels, looking at the other, that 'I had been faced by my own reflection in the depths of a sombre and immense mirror'. The tale is psychologically gripping in the way it shows how, for the captain, 'the dual working of my mind distracted me almost to insanity'. The story seems to express how Conrad himself feels 'distracted' by the division in his own mind. On the one hand he respects authority, on the other he is fascinated by rebellion.

Writing of his own art Conrad shows a tormentedly divided mind. On the one hand he expresses a huge artistic ambition, sounding like a prophet rather than a novelist, when he offers his work as 'a single-minded attempt to render the highest kind of truth to the visible universe by bringing to light the truth, manifold and one, underlying its every aspect', and talks of his 'task' as being 'by the power of the written word to make you hear, to make you feel – it is, before all, to make you *see*' (preface to *The Nigger of the 'Narcissus'*). On the other hand there is the Conrad of repeated nervous breakdowns, who expresses in his personal writings a sense of the futility and unreality of the task of writing – even a letter:

> Even writing to a friend – to a person one has heard, touched, drunk with, quarrelled with – does not give one a sense of reality. All is illusion – the words written, the mind at which they are aimed, the truth they are intended to express, the hands that will hold the paper, the eyes that will glance along the lines. Every image floats in a sea of doubt – and the doubt itself is lost in an unexplored universe of incertitudes.

This extraordinary variety of contradictions: masculine and feminine, simple and subtle, authoritarian and rebellious, publicly confident and privately agonized, helps to make sense of Conrad's own statement in a letter that '*Homo duplex*' (double man) 'has in my case more than one meaning'.

What were the roots of Conrad's divided nature? His Polish background provides some clues to the enduring contradiction of his emotional and political loyalties. He

The Korzeniowskis.
Conrad's father
Apollo, uncle Robert
and grandfather
Theodor.

was born Joseph Konrad Nalecz Korzeniowski on 3 December 1857 at Berdycowz in Polodia, a part of the Ukraine which had belonged to Poland until the partition of 1793 but which was now governed by Tsarist Russia. The middle name Konrad, which he chose in later life to use as a surname, probably refers to the romantic, nationalist hero of the great nineteenth-century Polish poet Mickiewicz's epic poem *Konrad Wallenrod*. Conrad's later gesture of highlighting this Polish connection carries, as we shall see, certain overtones of guilt and irony.

A Polish peasant at the end of the nineteenth century. Conrad's father campaigned to improve the lot of the peasantry while belonging to the class that ruled them.

Conrad's parents belonged to the Polish land-owning gentry who very much thought of themselves as an aristocracy, keeping alive soldierly, chivalric and nationalist values. This Polish gentry in the Ukraine were in the curious double position of being both an oppressed and an oppressing minority; they were politically dominated by Russia as part of the Russian empire, but as landowners themselves had economic power over the Ukrainian peasantry who were mainly non-Polish. The families of Conrad's parents – the Korzeniowskis and the Brobrowskis – broadly represented the two strands in the Polish response to Russian rule. The former favoured a continual radical resistance, while the latter hoped that holding back from protest would lead to a gradual reform.

Conrad aged three in 1861, the year of his father's arrest.

His uncle on his mother's side, Stefan Brobrowski, was a member of the provisional government and died in a duel with a political opponent in 1862. On his father's side his uncle, Robert Korzeniowski, was killed in the Polish rising against Russia in 1863. Another uncle, Hilary Korzeniowski, was exiled to Siberia in 1863 and died there ten years later. Conrad's father, Apollo Nalecz Korzeniowski, was involved in a range of political agitation and what we would now call 'dissident' literary activity. He was a playwright and a poet who wrote on religious and patriotic themes, translated Shakespeare, Victor Hugo and Alfred de Vigny and organized peasant education. He urged people not to vote in elections and organized mass demonstrations. Martial law was declared in 1861 and Apollo helped set up the 'Central National Committee'. This illegal organization was the controlling force in Polish opposition to Russian rule until 1863 when the Russians crushed a wave of uprisings.

Fighting at Vengrov during the abortive Polish uprising against Russian rule in 1863, in which Conrad's uncle Robert was killed.

Apollo was found guilty and sent into exile to the distant Russian province of Vologda, his wife Evelina choosing to accompany him with their four-year-old son. For the next three years the family lived in the appalling conditions of what was in effect a concentration camp. In a letter of 1862 Apollo wrote of the conditions:

> The climate consists of two seasons of the year: a white winter and a green winter. The white winter lasts nine-and-a half months and the green one two-and-a-half. We are now on the onset of the green winter; it has already been raining ceaselessly for twenty-one days and that's how it will be until the end . . . the population is a nightmare, disease-ridden corpses.

This might remind us of 'Heart of Darkness', in which Conrad depicts the 'nightmare' of Africans oppressed by their Belgian colonial rulers. The climate and general deprivation affected Conrad whose health, nervous and physical, was weak for the rest of his life. It proved fatal to Evelina who died of tuberculosis when Conrad was seven.

Conrad aged four at Moscow in 1862, the year he accompanied his parents into exile.

He was then separated from his father, sent back to Poland and placed in the care of his uncle Tadeusz, who constantly reminded his nephew of what he would represent as his father's irresponsibility and the tragic waste of his mother's life. Five years later, when Conrad was thirteen, his father, health and spirit broken, was sent home and died within the year.

This series of traumatic experiences can be seen to have developed in Conrad a painfully complicated attitude to politics. He must have been deeply affected by the heroic nature of his parents' protest, yet he had seen their idealism result only in the miseries of exile and in both their deaths. In later years Conrad adopted a conservative, indeed reactionary, political stance and his fiction pours great scorn upon agitators such as the repulsive Donkin in *The Nigger of the 'Narcissus'*. He is habitually scornful of revolutionary ideas and political thought generally, famously declaring in a letter that he had 'no creed'. Yet at the same time, though he is suspicious of his characters when they express political ideals such as the radical ideas of the 'Future of the Proletariat' in *The Secret Agent*, Conrad himself uses his novels to explore the same ideas.

Conrad aged fifteen in 1873, the year he left Poland for a sea career.

Marseilles in 1895, where the young Conrad indulged in expensive escapades and then began his career at sea.

Such a background might in itself explain why, by the age of sixteen, Conrad was eager for the career at sea which, since Poland had no sea coast at this time, would inevitably mean long absences from his native country. Having devoured in childhood the works of Captain Marryat and Robert Louis Stevenson, and Hugo's *Toilers of the Sea*, Conrad had been inspired, like his hero Lord Jim, by 'the sea-life of light literature'. But this romantic strain in his ambition was coupled with an urgently practical one. In Russian Poland, as the son of a convict, he was eligible for twenty-five year's service in the Russian army, and this danger intensified when Tadeusz failed to secure Austrian citizenship for him in 1872. In 1874 he boarded the Vienna Express on his way to the sea at Marseilles 'as

a man might get into a dream'. In *Some Reminiscences* (1912) he wrote of the difficulty of breaking these ties:

> ... having broken away from my origins under a storm of blame from every quarter which had the merest shadow of a right to voice an opinion, removed by great distance from such natural affections as were still left to me, and even estranged, in a measure, from them by the totally unintelligible nature of the life which had seduced me so mysteriously from my allegiance.

The idea of being 'seduced' from his 'allegiance' gives weight to the argument popular with Conrad's biographers that he felt that in opting for the life of a seaman and exile he was betraying the national cause for

'*... a swarm of strange men, clambering up her sides, took possession of her in the name of the sordid earth. She had ceased to live*' (The Nigger of the 'Narcissus'). *Landing cargo at Fresh Wharf, London Bridge, 1874.*

The Otago, *on which Conrad had his first and only command in 1882. The chief mate's obsession with the previous master's madness and death on board inspired* The Shadow-Line.

which both his parents had died. Considered in this light his later life and writing can be seen as centrally concerned with the guilt that resulted from this crucial desertion. One persuasive piece of evidence that has been put forward for this view, is that the word 'jump', repeatedly used in *Lord Jim* for Jim's crucial act of seeming cowardice and betrayal when he deserts his ship, is the word Conrad uses to describe leaving Poland, 'I verily believe mine was the only case of a boy of my nationality and antecedents taking a, so to speak, standing jump out of his racial surroundings and associations.'

Over and over again, most explicitly in *The Mirror of the Sea* (1906) and *A Personal Record* (1912), Conrad meditates on the profound meaning his sea-life held for him. The most subtle treatment of the theme is the late novel *The Shadow-Line* (1917), a story based on Conrad's first and only command on the *Otago* in 1888. In one scene the new young captain meditates on the responsibilities of his role, but is strengthened by the thought that he forms part of a dynasty, or line or rulers, who keep alive a 'traditional point of view on life'. We get an impression of what must have been Conrad's own feeling of relief on joining the merchant service. He had abandoned the dangerous inheritance of the political struggles of the Polish aristocracy to ally himself to a perhaps less oppressive kind of tradition and duty.

Deep within the tarnished ormolu frame, in the hot half-light sifted through the awning, I saw my own face propped between my hands. And I stared back at myself with the perfect detachment of distance, rather with curiosity than with any other feeling, except of some sympathy for this latest representative of what for all intents and purposes was a dynasty; continuous not in blood, indeed, but in its experience, in its training, in its conception of duty, and in the blessed simplicity of its traditional point of view on life.

It struck me that this quietly staring man, whom I was watching, both as if he were myself and somebody else, was not exactly a lonely figure. He had his place in a line of men whom he did not know, of whom he had never heard; but who were fashioned by the same influences, whose souls in relation to their humble life's work had no secrets for him.

Peter O' Toole as Lord Jim in the film version of the storm scene. Conrad uses Jim's desertion of his ship to explore the nature of cowardice and moral integrity.

Gambling at Monte Carlo, c.1895. Conrad attempted suicide after losing 800 francs at the tables. His guardian complained, 'Where is there thought, prudence, deliberation??? ... Where is effort to diminish the faults of committed absurdities by thoughtful and tactful behaviour?'

When the captain of 'The Secret Sharer' had imagined that he was looking in a mirror, we sensed that he was inwardly divided because the role he had to fulfil was opposed to the needs of his own nature. Here the captain looks at his own image with calmness and the sense that there is no real contradiction between his personality and his role as captain. But this sense of assurance is soon upset. Having achieved a kind of inner stability through contemplating the greatness of a dynasty of which he is now a part, the captain is to discover that the captain he replaces was a dangerous lunatic who had endangered the lives of all on board. He had kept the ship in a fever-ridden port while he conducted an affair onshore, secretly selling the ship's medicine supply to finance it. It is typical of Conrad, and another of his contradictions, that his narrators continually assert the 'blessed simplicity' of 'a traditional point of view on life', in novels that show his characters undergoing trials that seem anything but 'simple' and 'traditional'.

For the next three and a half years Conrad was, in effect, apprentice to a French shipowner and learnt seamanship on a number of voyages to the West Indies and elsewhere. He also reacted against the constraints of his miserable childhood in a number of financial and romantic escapades. He ran up gambling debts, got involved in gun-running for the Carlist cause in Spain and apparently had a disastrous love affair. Matters came to a head in 1878, the truth of which has only recently been discovered. It had been thought that Conrad injured himself in a duel at this time, but a letter Tadeusz wrote to a friend in 1879 gives another version of events:

> ... wishing to improve his finances [Conrad] tries his luck in Monte Carlo and looses the 800fr. he has borrowed. Having managed his affairs so excellently he returns to Marseilles and one fine evening invites his friend the creditor to tea, and before his arrival attempts to take his life with a revolver. (Let this detail remain between us, as I have been telling everyone that he was wounded in a duel. From you I neither wish to nor should keep it a secret.) The bullet goes *durch* [through] and *durch* near his heart without damaging any vital organ.

The wool clipper Loch Etive, *on which Conrad served as officer on a voyage to Sydney in 1880–81. '... neither the tone, nor the manner, nor yet the drift of Captain S--'s remarks addressed to myself did ever, by the most strained interpretation, imply a favourable opinion of my abilities.'* (The Mirror of the Sea)

At the age of twenty-one Conrad signed on with an English ship, ferrying goods between Lowestoft (pictured here) and Constantinople.

The scarcity of evidence surrounding Conrad's suicide attempt means that our position in attempting to speculate about it is pretty much that of the newspaper report of Winnie's suicide in *The Secret Agent* (1907), which admits that 'An impenetrable mystery seems destined to hang for ever over this act of madness or despair'. We do know that suicide, and particularly its challengingly 'mysterious' aspects, becomes a central concern of Conrad's fiction. In *Lord Jim* (1900) Conrad writes a long paragraph detailing the numerous professional successes of one Captain Brierly, who has been awarded an inscribed gold chronometer and silver-mounted binoculars in recognition of the excellence of his seamanship. Whose 'self-satisfaction presented . . . to the world a surface as hard as granite'. The last sentence informs us 'He committed suicide very soon after'. The reader is challenged to fill in the gap Conrad has left between Brierly's life of evident professional achievement and formidable self-assurance, and the suicide that ends it. Conrad leaves it to us to ponder whether the two cannot be linked, or whether the suicide is in some sense a natural outcome of such a life.

A significant ingredient of his despair at this time must have been his discovery that his ambition of joining the French Merchant Marine was blocked by his being liable to military service in a foreign country. His prospects brightened, however, when he discovered that the British service had no such barriers. He signed on with the English freighter *Mavis*, ferrying coal and linseed oil between Lowestoft and Constantinople. Thus it was rather through necessity than the long-established resolve he was later to claim, that at the age of twenty-one Conrad came under the Red Ensign, which he described in *A Personal Record* as the 'symbolic, protecting warm bit of bunting flung wide upon the seas, and destined for so many years to be the only roof over my head'.

This image suggests some of the spirit of ardent patriotism typical of late Victorian England. However, when Conrad expresses such sentiments they almost always create unease in the reader. Conrad became a British citizen in 1886 and had committed himself to Britain at a time when its empire dominated the world economically and politically and when nationalist and imperialist feeling ran high. This move can be seen to be of greater and more hidden psychological significance to

Victoria's Golden Jubilee procession in 1887, the year before Conrad became a British citizen, was a focus for the nationalist sentiments over which Conrad had divided feelings.

Conrad than even his commitment to sea life. The imagination which so powerfully denounces the sordid economics of 'material interests' in *Nostromo* (1904) and the 'scramble for loot' of a Western empire in 'Heart of Darkness' (1899), could not but feel an uneasy relation with his adopted culture and its values. Like the dutiful public Edwardian he became, he paid homage to the 'national spirit' in the last pages of *The Mirror of the Sea*, but in a way that is more expressive of the excruciating effort to believe in nationalist sentiments than it is of those sentiments themselves:

> In this ceaseless rush of shadows and shades, that , like the fantastic forms of clouds cast darkly upon the waters on a windy day, fly past us to fall headlong below the hard edge of an implacable horizon, we must turn to the national spirit, which, superior in its force and continuity to good and evil fortune, can alone give us the feeling of an enduring existence and of an invincible power against the fates.

The proclamation of Queen Victoria as Empress of India at Delhi, 1877.

It would be difficult to imagine a more powerful beginning followed by a more unpersuasive conclusion. The 'national spirit' sounds a fake and insubstantial thing in

the face of that 'ceaseless rush of shadows and shades' Conrad imagines so vividly. Perhaps hidden too deep for Conrad openly to acknowledge is the feeling that various 'national spirits' were precisely the forces that were driving Europe, in the years before the First World War, over 'the hard edge of an implacable horizon'.

In sixteen years at sea Conrad rose to qualify as third, second and first mate before finally, in 1886, attaining the rank of master in the British merchant marine. Particularly memorable experiences amongst his voyages to the Atlantic and Pacific, the Americas and the coasts and seas of the East form the core of the narratives of *Almayer's Folly*, *Youth*, *The Nigger of the 'Narcissus'*, *The Shadow-Line* and the sea-career of Lord Jim.

Conrad's adventuring years as a seaman, and in a deep sense the whole unreflective youthful phase of his life, was effectively brought to an end with his Congo experience of 1890. The central African territory was part of the empire ruled by Belgium, and Conrad was employed as the captain of a river steamboat plying between the trading posts Belgium had established in order to export ivory for the European trade in luxury goods. For Conrad

The Tilkhurst, *on which Conrad served as a second mate. He was proud to recall Captain Blake's promise, 'If you happen to be in want of employment, remember that as long as I have a ship you have a ship, too.'* (The Mirror of the Sea).

the fulfilment of a boyhood ambition to explore the Congo and its mysterious river of the same name turned into a nightmare experience of Western exploitation. He witnessed at first hand the swindling, brutality and atrocities that the Belgian regime committed against the native population which the British Consul in the Congo Roger Casement, made notorious in a famous report of 1904. Its shocking revelations helped turn the tide of popular imperialist sentiment in Britain. Casement asked Conrad to help him compile his report, but Conrad declined. This refusal could be taken to suggest that Conrad could only express the intense feelings of horror and disillusion his experience had created by turning them into fiction such as 'Heart of Darkness' (*see* Chapter 4). Casement and Conrad's texts remain two of the great documents of the decline of the Victorian world view.

In later years Conrad was to state that before this experience he 'was a perfect animal'. In the Congo Conrad crossed his own 'shadow-line' dividing youth and maturity, becoming thereafter – in a term which carries ominous weight when used of the troubled crew of the *Narcissus* – 'self-conscious'. The result of this newly disillusioned and self-conscious personality was the career Conrad now embarked on as a writer. The Congo had killed off the spirit of adventure in him and the novels and short stories which he was now to write had as a major theme (as in 'Youth', 'Amy Foster' and *Lord Jim*) the central character's initial adventuring optimism being threatened by disillusion and self doubt.

Conrad married in 1896. In a letter to a Polish relative he described his fiancée with the eccentric and unromantic off-handedness which was to characterize their marriage:

I announce solemnly (as the occasion demands) to dear Aunt Gabryina and to you both that I am getting married. No one can be more surprised at it than myself. However I am not frightened at all, for as you know, I am accustomed to an adventurous life and to facing terrible dangers. Moreover, I have to avow that my betrothed does not give the impression of being at all dangerous. Jessie is her name; George her surname. She is a small, not at all striking-looking person (to tell the truth alas – rather plain!) who nevertheless is very dear to me. When I met her a year and a half ago she was earning her living in the City as a 'Typewriter' in an American business office of the 'Caligraph' company.

Aspects of colonial rule in the Congo. **Left** *A photograph from the evidence collected by Roger Casement for his notorious report on Belgian atrocities. 'Black shapes crouched, lay, sat between the trees against the trunks...in all the attitudes of pain, abandonment and despair.' ('Heart of Darkness').* **Below** *The refined leisure of colonial agents, like Conrad's spruce Congo accountant. '...in the great demoralisation of the land he kept up his appearance.'*

His second novel *An Outcast of the Islands* was published in the month of his marriage. *Almayer's Folly*, the manuscript of which accompanied him in the Congo, had been published the year before.

Edward Garnett, Conrad's friend and publisher, wrote that his 'Ultra-nervous personality appeared to make matrimony extremely hazardous'. Depressive and introverted – especially during the painful periods of composition – Conrad would complain of being *'absolument embourbé'* (completely stuck), of *'les nerfs! les nerfs!'* (bad nerves) and that everything was *'noir, noir, noir'* (black). Conrad's depressions and sense of the futility of

Conrad's son Borys with his pet rabbits.

A letter from Conrad to Edward Garnett, 9 April 1896, honeymooning at Ile-Grande, Brittany. 'I have written 15 pages of the dullest trash!'

his writing must have stemmed partly from his striving to achieve success as a writer at a time when the more robust sentiments of bestselling authors such as Rudyard Kipling, John Galsworthy and Arnold Bennett, and many much less gifted, were popular. Jessie gives one example of his moods when she describes to a doctor friend his state of collapse on completion of *Under Western Eyes* (1910):

> The novel is finished, but the penalty has to be paid. Months of nervous strain have ended in a complete nervous breakdown. Poor Conrad is very ill and Dr Hackney says it will be a long time before he is fit for anything requiring mental exertion. I know both you and dear Mrs Meldrum will feel every sympathy with him. There is the M.S. complete but uncorrected and his fierce refusal to let even I touch it. It lays on a table at the foot of his bed and he lives mixed up in the scenes and holds converse with the characters.
>
> I have been up with him night and day since Sunday week and he, who is usually so depressed by illness, maintains he is not ill, and accuses the Dr and I of trying to put him into an asylum.

Jessie, Borys, Conrad and a friend, Ellen Anderson, in the garden at Capel House, Kent in 1914.

Opposite *Postcard of Ivy Walls, Essex, where Conrad and Jessie moved in 1897. From here Conrad wrote to Garnett of 'At times thinking the world* has *come to an end – at others convinced that it has not yet come out of chaos'.*

This description illustrates how in these later years spent in essentially uneventful retirement in houses in Kent and Bedfordshire – the most significant outward events being the births of his sons Alfred Borys in 1898, and John Alexander in 1906 – Conrad lived with exhausting vitality the life of his own fiction-making, but was disengaged from his actual roles as husband and father. There is a famous anecdote illustrating a quite literal and domestic instance of that quality of appearing 'aloof and apart' which Virginia Woolf noted in his 'genius'. He would allow Jessie and the boys to travel with him in a train compartment, but only if they pretended not to be with him, and was once most annoyed when the evidently sorely tried Jessie needed him to help with the luggage.

The years from *The Nigger of the 'Narcissus'* (1897) to *Under Western Eyes* (1910) produced Conrad's finest work. One biographer has compared Conrad's literary career in this financially insecure but artistically flourishing period to that of the hero of Henry James's short story 'The Next Time'. Pressurized by his family commitments the writer tries ever harder to write in the popular manner he feels will provide a money-spinning bestseller, only to find that every 'next time' he produces a work more brilliant and unsaleable than the last. Only with *Chance* (1912) and *Victory* (1914) did Conrad achieve genuinely popular successes that gave him perhaps the first financial security of his life, but these novels are generally taken to represent

POST CARD

O
2

COMMUNICATION | ADDRESS ONLY

Ivy Walls – our first farmhouse home where B was born in 1898. in Essex. We lived there just a year. Written there. *Karain*. *Return*. Part of *Rescue* (not finished yet) and last of all *Youth* which story is exactly a month younger than Borys.

a decline in his powers. The works of the years immediately prior to his death in 1924 such as *The Arrow of Gold* (1919) and *The Rescue* (1920) revisit the themes of youthful adventure but, lacking the buoyancy and conviction essential to romance, slip into what Virginia Woolf called 'stiff melodrama'.

The crisis of conviction which produced such stiffness also produced, in *The Shadow-Line*, the masterpiece of this late period. This short novel presents a sombre retrospect

of Conrad's life and the enduring concerns of his fiction. A young captain is languishing on shore feeling his life to be merely a 'dreary, prosaic waste of days' and that there is 'nothing original, nothing new, startling, informing to expect from the world'. He is released from this 'menace of emptiness' by his appointment to a captaincy which he excitedly expects will be the exacting 'test of manliness, of temperament, of courage, of fidelity – and of love' he craves. He is, in fact, tested far more severely than he could have imagined. A fever takes hold of the crew while the ship remains so becalmed that her canvas hangs like granite. The stricken mate becomes morbidly obsessed with the previous captain who had died damning all on board, and fears that the ship will perish unless she braves the curse by passing over the latitude at sea (the shadow-line) where he was buried. The captain feels his sense of purpose and sanity erode, 'I felt the inexpungable strength of common sense being insidiously menaced by this grotesque, by this insane delusion'. The captain does eventually brave the threats of the mate's morbidity, the fever and the journey's physical trials. Above all he faces the oppressive dreariness of his own state of mind and the dispiriting ordeal of the ship becoming becalmed, which Conrad uses to symbolize it. The ship crosses the shadowy latitude and finds port but not before Conrad has faced, with a fortitude comparable to that of his captain, the full experience of isolation and negation. At one moment the captain feels himself utterly isolated by the night's darkness:

In one stride I penetrated it. Such must have been the darkness before creation. It had closed behind me. I knew I was invisible to the man at the helm. Neither could I see anything. He was alone, I was alone. Every man was alone where he stood. And every form was gone too, spar, sail, fittings, rails; everything was blotted out in the dreadful smoothness of that absolute night.

In a passage such as this we can sense what D.H. Lawrence meant when he wrote that he could not forgive Conrad 'for being so sad, and for giving in'. We can also understand what the critic Terry Eagleton means when he says that Conrad expresses with great vividness a feeling characteristic of his time, that sees individuals as frighteningly isolated one from another.

Opposite *D. H. Lawrence, who said that he could not forgive Conrad for 'being so sad'.*

Trench warfare at Neuve Chapelle, 1915. The Shadow-Line *is presented as a homage to the war generation, 'To Borys and all others who like himself have crossed in early youth the shadow-line of their generation, with love.'*

The severity of Conrad's pessimism here is doubly disturbing when we realize that *The Shadow-Line* also has a clear relevance to the moment when it was written. The novel is autobiographical in the sense that it offers both a look back at Conrad's own early self, at a time when he was seeking direction, and also expresses the world-weary perspective of the elderly author who complains of his own imagination becoming, like the ship in the novel, agonizingly 'stuck'. In addition to these autobiographical meanings, the novel creates in the captain's experience an analogy with the ordeals of the contemporary generation of youth who, like Conrad's own son Borys, were at the time of writing fighting in the trenches of the First World War. The war itself was like an immense slough in which the whole of Europe foundered and which was the test of a whole generation's self-possession. In contrast to Lawrence's view of his 'giving in', Conrad praised the French writer Anatole France for wishing men to 'believe and hope, preserving in our activity the consoling illusion of power and intelligent purpose', and, having taken its full look at the worst, the novel dramatizes the long haul towards a hard-won optimism.

Conrad's son Borys in his uniform as a second lieutenant. He served three years at the Flanders front before being sent home in 1918 to recover from the effects of poison gas and shell-shock.

Two final quotations from Marlow, the narrator whom Virginia Woolf describes as Conrad's second, subtle self, will provide us with clues as to how to read Conrad's text and characters. In *Chance* he discusses the nature of his 'understanding' in a way that provides us with a clue:

'Luckily, people, whether mature or not mature (and who is ever mature?), are for the most part quite incapable of understanding what is happening to them: a merciful provision of nature to preserve an average amount of sanity for working purposes in this world . . . '

'But we, my dear Marlow, have the inestimable advantage of understanding what is happening to others . . . Is that too a provision of nature? And what is it for? Is it that we may amuse ourselves gossiping about each other's affairs? You, for instance seem – '

'I don't know what I seem,' Marlow silenced me, 'and surely life must be amused somehow. It would still be a very respectable provision if it were only for that end. But from that same provision of understanding, there springs in us compassion, charity, indignation, the sense of solidarity; and in minds of any largeness an inclination to that indulgence which is next to affection.'

The Torrens, *one of the most famous ships of the day, on which Conrad served as first mate in 1891–92. It was on this journey that he carried the manuscript of his first novel and met the novelist, John Galsworthy.*

In *Lord Jim*, Marlow is fascinated by the enigmatic figure of Jim who seems to challenge his notions of character, and of truth itself:

I can't explain to you who haven't seen him and who hear his words only at second hand the mixed nature of my feelings. It seemed to me that I was being made to comprehend the inconceivable – and I know of nothing to compare with the discomfort of such a sensation. I was made to look at the convention that lurks in all truth and on the essential sincerity of falsehood. He appealed to all sides at once – to the side turned perpetually to the light of day, and to the other side of us which, like the other hemisphere of the moon, exists stealthily in perpetual darkness, with only a fearful ashy light falling at times on the edge. He swayed me. I own to it, I own up. The occasion was obscure, insignificant – what you will: a lost youngster, one in a million – but then he was one of us; an incident as completely devoid of importance as the flooding of an ant heap, and yet the mystery of his attitude got hold of me as though he had been an individual in the forefront of his kind, as if the obscure truth involved were momentous enough to affect mankind's conception of itself . . .

Here again are striking contradictions. Marlow believes that the stories he tells should create in the reader both 'indignation' and 'indulgence', which seem opposite responses. The history of Lord Jim seems to him to be both 'completely devoid of importance' and to express a 'truth ... momentous enough to affect mankind's conception of itself'. In the stories which are discussed in the following chapters, *The Nigger of the 'Narcissus'*, *The Secret Agent* and 'Heart of Darkness', we will find that such divided responses are the very basis of Conrad's art.

Conrad c.1911.

2

The Nigger of the 'Narcissus'

In the *Mirror of the Sea* Conrad elaborates on the theme of the preface to *The Nigger of the 'Narcissus'* that the artist's task is 'to make you *see*',

> To see! To see! – that is the craving of the sailor, as of the rest of blind humanity. To have his path made clear to him is the aspiration of every human being in our beclouded and tempestuous existence.

For Conrad the desire 'to see' carries the wish to find a clear and purposeful direction for one's life and, the maritime context implies, the particular environment and values that make the journey possible. After what we might think of as Conrad's 'beclouded' and 'tempestuous' youth of bereavement, exile and political oppression it is perhaps easy to understand why the principle of duty he found in the merchant service appealed so strongly. Here perhaps he glimpsed a 'clear path' for his life in a conservative view of conduct that stressed the dignity of discipline and endurance.

As Conrad's first sea novel after his abandonment of the merchant service *The Nigger of the 'Narcissus'* is a particularly important test case for him to see if he can find a continuity of values between the two careers. The emphasis in the preface upon writing as a 'task' (a term used five times) 'investigating the dark corners of the earth', the 'far-off' nature of success and the necessity of strength to undertake the 'travel', all suggest that he here

believes that the disciplined virtues of seamanship are also those of novel writing. But a preface is not a novel. In 'Heart of Darkness' Marlow is fascinated by a book he finds in the jungle on the breaking strains of ships' cables. Conrad's novels are themselves about breaking strains; those of his characters who undergo extreme physical, but mainly mental, ordeals and also of the values Conrad brings to his writing from his seamanship which are similarly tested, troubled and – sometimes – found wanting.

As the *Narcissus* sets sail on its voyage from Bombay to London a psychological drama develops amongst the dominant members of the crew which threatens their 'solidarity' – a term Conrad singles out for praise in the novel's famous preface. The ship's name recalls that of the figure of Greek legend who died pining for love of himself having become obsessed with his own reflection. The myth appealed to Conrad because of the theme of the destructiveness of self-absorption. *The Nigger of the 'Narcissus'* focuses on the antagonistic relations between the three dominant members of the crew and how they each relate to its vital solidarity: Donkin and Jimmy Wait, who appear to threaten it and Singleton, who appears to preserve it.

Bombay port, from where Conrad sailed on the Narcissus *to Dunkirk in 1884, using the event for his first sea-novel. 'Most of the personages I have portrayed actually belonged to the crew of the* Narcissus, *including the admirable Singleton...Archie, Belfast and Donkin.'*

Narcissus, the mythical figure who, like Jimmy Wait, on the ship of that name, languishes in self-absorption.

The narrator's attitude to Donkin, and the set of values that dominate his telling of the tale, are made clear in his assessment of him as 'the creature that knows all about his rights, but knows nothing of courage, of endurance and of the unexpressed faith, of the unspoken loyalty that knits together a ship's company'. Donkin is held up as the enemy of 'the solidarity . . . in toil, in joy, in hope, in uncertain fate, which binds men to each other and all mankind to the visible world', praised in the preface. The first we hear from him is an argument he is having with the likeable Belfast. Belfast is all for crewmen 'sticking together' and his attitude contrasts with Donkin who aggressively insists that 'I can look after my rights'. The narrator's near neurotic attack upon Donkin for his disruptive insistence on his 'rights' and desire to 'kick up a bloomin' row' – he is described as a 'filthy object' 'incredibly delapidated', his 'inefficient carcass' 'scratched, spat upon, pelted with unmentionable filth' – reflects how keen Conrad is to attack the liberal attitudes Donkin embodies.

In this respect the novel reinforces the anti-democratic theme typical of English sea fiction. In Captain Marryat's hugely popular *Mr Midshipman Easy*, favourite boyhood reading of Conrad's, the easy-going midshipman gradually learns through commitment to the service the folly of his youthful infatuation with the libertarian ideals he had picked up from Tom Paine's *The Rights of Man*. Conrad's novel lacks the comic quality of Marryat's and Donkin is shown to be incapable of any improvement.

The other internal threat to the crew's solidarity is that represented by the enigmatic ailing negro, Jimmy Wait. He languishes in his cabin claiming to be ill in such a way that no one can be sure, until his death on board, whether or not he is shamming. His disquieting presence stirs up a corrosive pity and anxiety amongst the crew. The ship's discipline is threatened when Belfast steals a fruit pie from the officers' store to tempt Jimmy's appetite. At another level, Jimmy's presence forces the crew to become morbidly self-conscious. Instead of singlemindedly devoting themselves to their work they begin to question the purpose of their own lives.

A sailor of the British Merchant Marine, 1860, the service Conrad joined in 1878.

This theme is a very complex one. In the novel's preface Conrad had explicitly stated that the role of art was to make 'the hands busy about the work of the earth ... pause for a look, for a sigh, for a smile – such is the aim, difficult and evanescent'. In other words, Conrad argues that art should force us away from our daily concerns to help us consider our lives. But Conrad is actually very anxious when this is the precise effect Jimmy has on the crew. Under his influence they become 'highly humanized, tender, complex, excessively decadent'. At one point the narrator says 'They were forgetting their toil. They were forgetting themselves'. One of the crucial questions Conrad's novels of seamanship help us to explore is whether our 'toil' really is 'ourself'. In 'Heart of Darkness' Conrad asks whether the work the modern world demands helps to fulfil or to destroy us.

Singleton's silent dedication to the ship seems to be an ideal example of how a man and his work can be in complete accord. His unreflective and nearly mystical absorption in his duties is held up for the reader's admiration as often as Donkin is for their disgust: 'he radiated unspeakable wisdom'. He receives Conrad's highest praise as one seafarer to another when in describing his 30 hours at the wheel in the storm the narrator simply states 'He steered with care'. Yet for all this, there are signs of strain in Conrad's efforts to admire him. Thus when the narrator praises Singleton's 'completed wisdom' the term seems an unsatisfying one. Conrad's novels very vividly express his belief that wisdom is too complicated a thing ever to be complete.

The narrator frequently pauses to praise the demands of sea life in ways that make it sound more like a religion than a job. But weaknesses and contradictions are never far from the surface when the narrator is at his most grandly assertive. Consider, for instance, the famous description of sea life opening Chapter 4:

On men reprieved by its disdainful mercy, the immortal sea confers in its justice the full privilege of desired unrest. Through the perfect wisdom of its grace they are not permitted to meditate at ease upon the complicated and acrid savour of existence. They must without pause justify their life to the eternal pity that commands toil to be hard and unceasing, from sunrise to sunset, from sunset to

sunrise; till the weary succession of nights and days tainted by the obstinate clamour of sages, demanding bliss and an empty heaven, is redeemed at last by the vast silence of pain and labour, by the dumb fear and the dumb courage of men obscure, forgetful and enduring.

This passage is curious in that it explicitly praises the demands of the seaman's life of labour for not allowing 'ease' during which he could meditate upon life, the awful meaninglessness of which seems obvious to the narrator. The preface, in marked contrast, had described the artist's task as precisely that of making the labourer pause in his work and consider his existence. Thus perhaps we can say that Conrad is torn between praising the current world of ceaseless 'pain and labour' together with the 'forgetfulness' it demands, and on the other hand wanting to examine and criticize it. In a sense *The Nigger of the 'Narcissus'* is Conrad's own meditation on what he sees as the 'complicated and acrid' aspects of life.

Opposite
Familiarity with night seascapes influenced Conrad's image of life as 'this ceaseless rush of shadows and shades'.

George Eliot, the nineteenth century novelist. Conrad broke with the tradition of the 'omniscient narrator,' typical of nineteenth-century fiction.

The helm of a merchant ship, 1910. Singleton spends 30 hours at the wheel during the storm in The Nigger of the 'Narcissus'.

Another complication in the novel is the uncertainty we feel over who is narrating it. Sometimes it is told by the 'omniscient' kind of narrator typical of nineteenth-century novels, such as those of George Eliot. This is not really an individual. It is more an all-seeing, all-knowing consciousness which can enter into and represent characters' states of mind and can stand apart from the action to offer clear interpretations of what is going on. At other times the narrator is clearly meant to be one of the crew, to which he refers as 'us' or 'we'. The passage already discussed praising 'pain and labour' would be a good example of a moment of omniscient narration. It is also an example of how omniscient narrators can often slip into a very grand and assertive explanation of events that seems quite distant from how we ourselves feel about the characters.

Another feature of this voice is that it offers us insights into the movement of the major characters' minds, often in ways that complicate our response to them. An example of this is the brilliant and disturbing passage evoking Jimmy's delirium after Donkin has refused him a drink of water, where the narration slips in and out of Jimmy's consciousness:

> He thought: that lunatic Belfast will bring me some water if I ask. Fool. I am very thirsty . . . It was very hot in the cabin, and it seemed to turn slowly round, detach itself from the ship, and swing out smoothly into a luminous, arid space where a black sun shone, spinning very fast. A place without any water! No water! A policeman with the face of Donkin drank a glass of beer by the side of an empty well, and flew away flapping vigorously. A ship whose masthead protruded through the sky and could not be seen, was discharging grain, and the wind whirled the dry husks in spirals along the quay of a dock with no water in it. He whirled along with the husks – very tired and light.

This is a fine example of Conrad's gift for representing extreme and tormented states of mind. For a moment we glimpse a side of Jimmy we had not suspected. To use the words Marlow used of Lord Jim, we see here his 'other side' which, for the majority of the novel, 'exists stealthily in perpetual darkness'. The intimacy of the experience here is strengthened by the use of the same image of 'husks' that Conrad uses later in the 'Author's Note' to *The Secret Agent* to describe his own mental exhaustion on completing *Nostromo*, 'as if I was left behind, aimless amongst mere husks of sensations'. Some of Conrad's own experience of tormenting mental pressure has gone into his creation of the disturbing and despised Jimmy.

How different an experience this sympathetic insight gives us of Jimmy to the narrator's initial depiction of him. Here the narrator seems only to see Jimmy from the outside. The hostility in his description seems more 'repulsive' than what it attempts to describe:

> He held his head up in the glare of the lamp – a head vigorously modelled into deep shadows and shining lights – a head powerful and misshapen with a tormented and flattened face – a face pathetic and brutal: the tragic, the mysterious, the repulsive mask of a nigger's soul.

Here the narrator refuses to understand Jimmy and heaps up weighty adjectives – always a tendency in Conrad – that seem rather to distance us from understanding him than bring us any nearer: 'pathetic', 'brutal', 'tragic', 'mysterious', 'repulsive'. At moments like this it seems to be Conrad's prose that wears a 'repulsive mask'. The fact that Jimmy is presented in such an inconsistent way, sometimes sympathetically and sometimes with hostility, suggests that he is as difficult for Conrad to pin down as he is for his fellow crew members.

Other instances of the insight that we associate with an omniscient narration would be when we learn that Captain Allistoun's 'secret ambition' is to make the *Narcissus* 'accomplish some day a brilliantly quick passage which would be mentioned in nautical papers'. This is significant since this piece of vanity threatens all on board

when he refuses to cut the mast when the ship is on its side after the storm. In a sense it is a piece of 'narcissism' more actually threatening to the crew than any 'symbolically' represented by Jimmy. Another instance would be the insight we have into Singleton's fears of old age and death in what seems close to his own form of expression: 'Old! It seemed to him he was broken at last . . . He had to take up at once the burden of all his existence, and found it almost too heavy for his strength. Getting old . . . and then?'

All these instances of 'interiorization' – when we look into a character's mind – give us rather different impressions of the characters from those we have previously had. Elsewhere the narrator stresses that Jimmy is menacingly mysterious, Allistoun is idealized and Singleton shown to be unreflective. It is one of the great elements of Conrad's writing that he keeps offering

*The modernist novelists, **right**, James Joyce, and **opposite**, Virginia Woolf. Conrad's experimentation with narrative paved the way for the modernist movement in fiction.*

us glimpses of his characters' inner lives – their delirium, follies or fears – which continually add to our understanding of them.

The mixture of different types of narration reflect Conrad's anxiety to see his story from all sides and get at the 'glimpse of truth' promised in the preface. It also suggests that Conrad was becoming dissatisfied with his omniscient narrator. In this sense *The Nigger of the 'Narcissus'* is a crucial work for the development of twentieth-century 'modernist' fiction, such as that of James Joyce or Virginia Woolf. Conrad's novel opens the way for these later writers, who replace the assured explanations of an omniscient narrator with a style that combines a shifting variety of narrating voices.

As the ship returns to the port and the novel moves to its close the narrator feels a need to sum up, and a particularly emphatic patriotic note is sounded. England is itself:

> a mighty ship . . . Carrying the burden of millions of lives
> . . . guarding priceless traditions and untold suffering . . .
> A great ship! . . A great ship mother of fleets and nations!
> The great flagship of the race!

The comparison between England and a ship suggests that the narrator hopes the social and political struggle on board the *Narcissus* can illuminate the problems of British social life, even in its military ('fleets') and colonial ('nations') aspects. While Conrad was writing the novel he offered it to W. E. Henley, who published it as a serial in his magazine *New Review*. Henley, like his friend Rudyard Kipling, wrote stridently patriotic verse (one poem contains the line 'Mother of Ships whose might / England my England / Is the fierce old sea's delight'). Perhaps

Millwall docks, on the River Thames, in 1868.

Conrad includes these clichéd patriotic sentiments more to please Henley and his circle of followers (known as the 'Henley regatta') than to express the real meaning of his novel.

The last pages of the novel, as the ship comes to port and the crew disperse, give us a whole variety of ways of responding to the strange meaning of her journey. There is an intense sadness for Conrad in the crew's hard-won solidarity finally being broken up. Characters who had seemed heroic when grappling with the demands of the storm, seem insecure and inadequate when returned to shore life. Singleton shortsightedly fumbles for his pay, so soon to be spent; Mr Baker strings out his final checks, reluctant to leave the deserted ship, not met by a sister, 'quite a lady', and brother-in-law who think a sailor relative beneath them; Charley is embarrassed by his mother's emotions and bribes her with money for drink; Belfast has a crying fit over Jimmy.

But these moving human actions are overshadowed by the mysterious workings of the wharf which is presented as if it were a mechanism. Conrad stresses how the ship is subdued by unnatural energies quite different from the human co-operation that brought her to port, 'A bridge broke in two before her, as if by enchantment; big hydraulic capstans began to move all by themselves as though animated by a mysterious and unholy spell'.

As the *Narcissus* docks, the unreality that at moments threatened to overwhelm Jimmy's mind seems actually to overwhelm the whole ship in the disconcerting and contradictory 'mad jumble' of dock life. Conrad uses the strange confusion of the port to suggest all the activity of the modern trading world:

Checking cargo unloaded from a merchant vessel, 1910.

Unloading tea at London docks, 1889.

Between high buildings the dust of all the continents soared in short flights; and a penetrating smell of perfumes and dirt, of spices and hides, of things costly and things filthy, pervaded the space, made for it an atmosphere precious and disgusting.

This novel so concerned with death ends with a kind of death for the ship herself as she docks:

The *Narcissus* came gently to her berth; the shadows of soulless walls fell upon her, the dust of all the continents leaped upon her deck, and a swarm of strange men, clambering up her sides, took possession of her in the name of the sordid earth. She had ceased to live.

The crew have been shown as diminished to mere insecure individuals. The *Narcissus* herself suffers a similar diminishment. Conrad had used her as a grand and complex symbol, but in port she becomes merely the carrier of a cargo. 'Shorn of the glory of her white wings,

55

she wound obediently after the tug through the maze of invisible channels'. As she enters a wharfscape more threatening and incomprehensible than that of Jimmy's delirium, his vision of a berthed ship eerily subdued and emptied becomes a reality:

> A mad jumble of begrimed walls loomed up vaguely in the smoke, bewildering and mournful like a vision of disaster ... soulless walls staring through hundreds of windows as troubled and dull as the eyes of over-fed brutes ... monstrous iron cranes crouched, with chains hanging from their long necks, balancing cruel-looking hooks over the decks of lifeless ships.

In marked contrast to the narrator's earlier grand assertion of the 'redeeming' nature of 'the vast silence of pain and labour', is the meaningless inhuman din of real labour, 'on all sides there was the clang of iron, the sound of mighty blows, shrieks, yells ... a noise of wheels rolling over stones, the thump of heavy things falling, the racket of feverish winches, the grinding of strained chains.'

In the sailor-narrator's farewell to his shipmates he

London docks in the 1890s. 'Lofty drifts of smoky vapours soiled it with livid trails; it throbbed to the beats of millions of hearts, and from it came an immense and lamentable murmur.' (The Nigger of the 'Narcissus').

56

interprets the journey as a kind of triumph, but not particularly convincingly:

> A gone shipmate, like any other man, is gone for ever; and I never met one of them again. But at times the spring-flood of memory sets with force up the dark River of the Nine Bends. Then on the waters of the forlorn stream drifts a ship – a shadowy ship manned by a crew of Shades. They pass and make a sign, in a shadowy hail. Haven't we, together and upon the immortal sea, wrung out a meaning from our sinful lives? Good-bye, brothers! You were . . . as good a crowd as ever fisted with wild cries the beating canvas of a heavy foresail; or tossing aloft, invisible in the night, gave back yell for yell to a westerly gale.

There is disillusion here as well as nostalgia; the 'dark River of the Nine Bends' of one sentence becomes merely a 'forlorn stream' in the next and in the image of a ghost-ship the narrator's vision seems tinged with a delirium like Jimmy's. The final image of the crew 'invisible in the night' yelling their 'wild cries' into the wind is like the whole novel, it gives an impression both of verve and of desperation.

3 *The Secret Agent*

The Nigger of the 'Narcissus' ended with a vision of London's docks 'bewildering and mournful, like a vision of disaster' into which the crew, now 'broken into knots' merges 'lost, alone, forgetful and doomed'. The reader is left with the sense that whatever ideal of 'solidarity' the narrator has gleaned from his story of the crew and their journey, the modern city is a more severe test of it than any Jimmy, Donkin or the sea could impose. The last thing we hear of London is its 'roar' which 'resembled the roar of topping breakers, merciless and strong, with a loud voice and cruel purpose'. The values that weathered a real storm at sea are perhaps to be sunk by the metaphorical waves of the city's hostility.

London. Piccadilly Circus.

What is left as a hint at the end of *The Nigger of the 'Narcissus'* is central to *The Secret Agent,* as we move from a novel concerned with solidarity to one essentially about secrecy; the corrosive effect on all values and relations of a merciless urban environment. The most active of the novel's agents, and the most secretive in its workings, is modern London itself. In Mr Verloc's queasy vision of London Conrad expresses a modern sense of the fragility of the individual's defences against an environment seen as incoherent and hostile:

T. S. Eliot. Conrad's work is a strong presence in Eliot's modernist poem The Waste Land.

> Then after slipping his braces off his shoulders he pulled up violently the venetian blind, and leaned his forehead against the cold window-panes – a fragile film of glass stretched between him and the enormity of cold, black, wet, muddy, inhospitable accumulations of bricks, slates, and stones, things in themselves unlovely and unfriendly to man.
> Mr Verloc felt the latent unfriendliness of all out of doors with a force approaching to positive bodily anguish.

In Mr Verloc Conrad creates a totally new character. In his nervous and ineffectual nature he expresses something central to twentieth-century literature's typically disillusioned and anti-heroic view of character. He anticipates T. S. Eliot's famous model for modern urban man, the equally tepid J. Alfred Prufrock, another frequenter of 'muttering retreats': 'Politic, cautious and meticulous;/. . .but a bit obtuse'. He is a prose version of one of those bowler-hatted petit bourgeois going about their business in an incongrous or sinister environment in a painting by the surrealist artists de Chirico or Magritte. (Like one of those little men he wears his hat indoors.)

Double Agent Mr Verloc has had the laziness of his routine shattered by one of his paymasters, Mr Vladimir, an *agent provocateur* sponsored by a foreign government. Vladimir has insisted that Verloc justify his salary by committing an outrage against the religion of modern times, science, by blowing up the Greenwich Observatory in London. So we might feel that in the quotation above his miserable view of the world has been coloured by his anxiety (particularly in this novel which, in another aspect of its modernity, stresses how one's state of mind can alter 'even the aspect of inanimate things'). But even when Mr Verloc is in a positively exuberant mood, in his morning walk in Hyde Park before meeting his paymaster, his

The Greenwich Observatory in 1895. It is Verloc's mission to blow it up. 'Such an outrage combines the greatest possible regard for humanity with the most alarming display of ferocious imbecility.' (The Secret Agent).

vision of the city is essentially of the same 'unfriendliness' and 'inhospitality', but now seen smugly from the point of view of the wealthy, who impose the unfriendliness and the authorities paid to police and preserve it:

> He surveyed through the park railings the evidences of the town's opulence and luxury with an approving eye. All these people had to be protected. Protection is the first necessity of opulence and luxury. They had to be protected; and their horses, carriages, houses, servants had to be protected in the heart of the city and the heart of the country; the whole social order favourable to their idleness had to be protected against the shallow enviousness of unhygienic labour.

Conrad develops the view of London as a place of extremes of wealth and poverty that was hinted at in the description in *The Nigger of the 'Narcissus'* of the city's 'penetrating smell . . . of things costly and of things filthy . . . an atmosphere precious and disgusting'. The disturbing suggestion that the sole function of the authorities is to protect the rich from the poor chimes in with the matter-of-fact explanation Verloc's wife Winnie gives to her anxious brother Stevie of the function of the police; '. . . so that them as have nothing shouldn't take anything away from them who have.'

Hyde Park, London, in 1907.

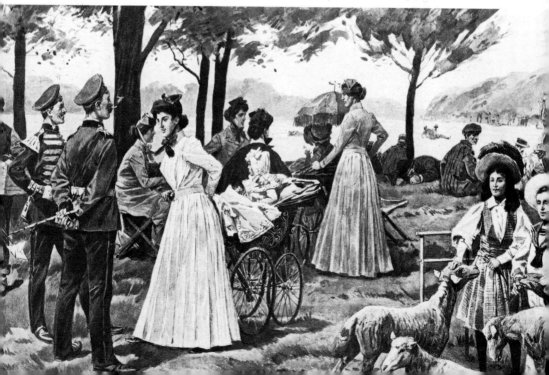

If we sensed in *The Nigger of the 'Narcissus'* that the 'unfriendliness' of the environment was as eternal as the elements because the sea was used to represent it, in *The Secret Agent* the environment is quite specifically London at the turn of the century, and the world's 'unfriendliness' is clearly an aspect of a particular culture. Conrad's depiction of urban life owes much to Dickens, especially Dickens at his darkest, for whom the city offers an image of innumerable secret lives massed together but essentially isolated. As the narrator of *A Tale of Two Cities* puts it:

> A solemn consideration, when I enter a great city by night, that every one of those darkly clustered houses encloses its own secret; that every room in every one of them encloses its own secret; that every beating heart in the hundreds of thousands of breasts is, in some of its imaginings, a secret to the heart nearest it!

In *The Secret Agent* Conrad has the same vision of individual lives lived in an untouchable isolation where emotions and communication are stunted. One connotation of his title is that everyone in the world he depicts is, in a sense, one who acts secretly. (Conrad is fond of titles that indicate the existence of a mystery while themselves being a mystery in the way they play on a variety of meanings – *The Secret Agent*, *The Shadow-Line*, 'The Secret Sharer', 'Heart of Darkness'.) In the London Conrad depicts, individuals are held in a sinister web of conspiratorial interdependence – revolutionaries and counter-revolutionaries, the liberal aristocracy and the petit bourgeoisie, the government and the police are all shown feeding off each others' existence – while at the same time each individual is emotionally 'as lonely and unsafe as though [he] had been situated in the midst of a forest'. Michaelis, leading light of the ineffectual anarchist cell the Future of the Proletariat, or FP, and former political prisoner, Mrs Verloc's mother and Mr Verloc himself are

Verloc muses, 'Protection is the first necessity of opulence and luxury...the whole social order favourable to their hygienic idleness had to be protected against the shallow enviousness of unhygienic labour.' (The Secret Agent). *Edwardian 'labour' and 'idleness'.*
Left, *a London slum, 1903.*
Above *Outside the retreat of the wealthy, the Ranelagh Club, 1907.*

all described with the repeated image of human lives being as shadowy and enclosed as claustrophobic rooms:

> [Michaelis] talked to himself, indifferent indeed to their presence, from the habit he had acquired of thinking aloud hopefully in the solitude of the four whitewashed walls of his cell, in the sepulchral silence of the great blind pile of bricks near a river, sinister and ugly like a colossal mortuary for the socially drowned.

> In the privacy of a four-wheeler, on her way to a charity cottage (one of a row) which by the exiguity of the dimensions and the simplicity of its accommodation, might well have been devised in kindness as a place of training for the still more straitened circumstances of the grave [Mrs Verloc's mother] was forced to hide from her own child a blush of shame.

> [Mr Verloc's] silence in itself had nothing startlingly unusual in this household, hidden in the shades of the sordid street seldom touched by the sun, behind the dim shop with its wares of disreputable rubbish.

At the turn of the century Britain became a haven for European radicals escaping persecution, like Conrad's Michaelis. **Below** *Stepniak, a Russian anarchist, in Bedford Park Lane, 1893.*

Conrad's story is based on an actual attempt to blow up the Greenwich Observatory in 1894, when the explosion did no damage but killed the perpetrator himself, the anarchist Martial Bourdin. Anarchist outrages were a popular anxiety for Edwardians, rather as modern terrorism is for us today, and the mad bomber was a stock villain in popular novels.

To commit the outrage, which his foreign paymaster organizes in order to discredit the revolutionary groups who will inevitably be blamed, Mr Verloc takes his wife's brother Stevie, an innocent near-idiot. Carrying the bomb, Stevie trips over a tree root and is killed by the explosion. The insipid Verloc expects the routine of his home life to continue unaffected by this outcome and returns home. Although Stevie's remains are unidentifiable, the police trace the Verlocs because of an address-label Winnie has conscientiously sewn into his jacket so he could be brought home if he were lost. When Winnie, whose life has been

The scene of the failed bomb attempt on the Greenwich Observatory, in February 1894, when Martial Bourdin, like Conrad's Stevie, blew himself up in Greenwich Park.

devoted to caring for her brother, discovers the truth of his death, including how the remains had to be collected in shovelfuls, she is shaken into her first ever dramatic action. She kills Verloc with a carving knife. She turns to one of his associates in FP, Ossipon, for help and when he robs and abandons her she literally becomes one of the 'socially drowned' by jumping from a Channel ferry.

Conrad often uses images of trading activities in order to take a critical look at the nature of his society. For example, the Verlocs' unassuming little shop in fact hides a number of strange deceptions. A non-committal window display mingles old revolutionary newspapers with photographs of dancing girls, and masks a business in what the men who embarrassedly buy sealed envelopes and magazines with 'promising titles' hope will be pornography. This itself fronts the Verlocs' typically proper bourgeois back parlour where Mr Verloc cultivates his domestic virtues, tended by Winnie. He assumes his wife is content and grateful for her position, whereas she has married him much against her inclinations in order to secure Stevie's future. Her dutifulness reflects anxiety rather than contentment. This 'humble abode of Mr Verloc's domestic happiness' is also the meeting place of a Marxist/anarchist cell, but the members' revolutionary views lead to much more talk and disagreement than actual activity. In turn this masks Mr Verloc's doubly deceptive undercover activities – he acts as an informer both for Mr Vladimir and Chief Inspector Heat of the special crimes department of the metropolitan police. Even this is not quite what it seems, as Verloc is usually too lazy and home-loving to carry out his duties. An apparently typical bourgeois marriage is built upon layers of deceit and shady dealing.

This illustrates how thoroughly sceptical Conrad is about any appearance of honesty in the contemporary world. This scepticism extends to the political ideals of the characters, ranging from the FP, who are 'open to all shades of revolutionary opinion' to the (presumably Russian) diplomat Mr Vladimir and the far-right American terrorist 'the Professor', and also including the police assistant commissioner, Chief Inspector Heat and the government representative, Sir Ethelred. Occasionally the reader feels that Conrad is too quick to dismiss his characters' ideas. During the meeting of the FP Michaelis

Opposite *A socialist speaking in Hyde Park, 1896.*

The political philosopher, Karl Marx, inspiration of Michaelis' politics, and, like him, a political refugee in England in the nineteenth century.

Opposite *This cartoon of 1892 reflects the same popular anxieties that Conrad draws on in* The Secret Agent – *that Britain's liberal attitude to political refugees left her open to anarchist terrorism.*

sums up the hugely influential view of history proposed by Karl Marx that 'history is made with tools, not with ideas; and everything is changed by economic conditions – art, philosophy, love, virtue – truth itself!' In *Nostromo* Conrad takes this Marxist idea very seriously. Episodes in the revolutionary history of a South American state stem more from the economic interests generated by the wealth of a silver mine than from political ideals or heroic actions. *Nostromo* is perhaps Conrad's greatest and most adventurous work because it looks very seriously at the idea central to modern thought that economics is the real force behind history, art, and even 'truth itself'.

RECKONING WITHOUT THEIR HOST.

Opposite *Conrad's friend and fellow novelist, H. G. Wells. The Secret Agent expresses Conrad's anxiety about the technological world prophesied in Wells's novels. 'He is a very original writer with a very individual judgement in all things and an astonishing imagination.'*

Conrad is sometimes cheaply scornful of his theorizing characters. He continually stresses how fat the Marxist Michaelis has become, reflecting his pampered life as the pet of a lady aristocrat. But at other times he criticizes their fixations with great skill. One such moment occurs when an embarrassing silence has fallen in the middle of one of Michaelis' tirades:

Mr Verloc, getting off the sofa with ponderous reluctance, opened the door leading into the kitchen to get more air, and thus disclosed the innocent Stevie, seated very good and quiet at a deal table, drawing circles, circles; innumerable circles, concentric, eccentric; a coruscating whirl of circles that by their tangled multitude of repeated curves, uniformity of form, and confusion of intersecting lines suggested a rendering of cosmic chaos, the symbolism of a mad art attempting the inconceivable.

The confusion of Stevie's 'mad art' is, in a sense, more articulate and deeply felt than the logic and rhetoric of the members of the FP. His obsession with circles perhaps expresses his anxious desire for an ideal social harmony explored in the famous 'cab-ride' chapter discussed below. His massing and intersecting of them as if in a 'cosmic chaos' reflects the social world of *The Secret Agent*, where essentially enclosed individuals meaninglessly clash and compete. In *Lord Jim* Stein suggests to Jim that if man is a 'masterpiece' then 'perhaps the artist was a little mad'. At any rate Stevie's 'good and quiet' occupation is the unknowing depiction of his own fate; he will be reduced to a 'tangled confusion' in the 'coruscating whirl' of an explosion. His 'mad art' is thus like Jimmy's delirious dream, in that it turns into reality.

In *The Secret Agent* Conrad clearly sees the modern world as menaced by dishonest political dogmas, anarchy and the worship of science and technology. The novel is dedicated to his friend and fellow novelist, H.G.Wells. Conrad calls him 'the historian of the ages to come' and Wells's fantasies of war and future technology, depicted in works such as *The War of the Worlds*, suggest something of the future that Conrad fears. In *The Secret Agent* Conrad questions how far the private values of sympathy and human ties can save us from such a future.

Conrad focuses on Stevie's intense sympathy for poverty and suffering and shows us how he grows in his

understanding of them. Winnie and Stevie accompany Mrs Verloc's mother in a horse-drawn cab to the miserable charity cottage where she has decided to end her days rather than remain a burden to Mr Verloc. She sacrifices her happiness under the delusion that Stevie's future will be more secure if less demands are made on Mr Verloc's kindness. During the journey Stevie becomes distressed by the haggard cabman whipping his equally wretched-looking horse. Stevie feels the animal's sufferings as if they were his own. But he achieves a crucial leap in understanding when he realizes that the cabman's cruelty is the result of the cruelty of society, which has created the man's desperate poverty. This enlargement of Stevie's understanding is shown in the use of the word 'poor'. He first uses it in an outburst of 'convulsive sympathy' for the stricken horse. At this stage Stevie's burning longings to alleviate suffering are futile because there is no understanding behind them. The only remedy he can imagine, which he is 'reasonable' enough to understand is impossible, is to take both horse and cabman consolingly to bed with him. But as the cabman explains his own need to feed his family, Stevie's use of the term expands:

'Its aspect was so profoundly lamentable, with such a perfection of macabre detail, as if it were the Cab of Death itself...' (The Secret Agent).

... Mrs Verloc, with that ready compassion of a woman for a horse (when she is not sitting behind him), exclaimed vaguely!

'Poor brute.'

Hanging back suddenly, Stevie inflicted an arresting jerk upon his sister.

'Poor! Poor!' he ejaculated appreciatively. 'Cabman poor, too. He told me himself.'

The Trinity Almshouses and Chapel.

Winnie is convinced that one should not 'look into things too much' and it is typical of her that when she uses the word 'poor' it merely means 'pathetic', and expresses only an easy and inactive sympathy. But for Stevie it now has the additional meaning of 'impoverished' and he shifts the emphasis from the sufferings of the animal to those of his driver. Cruelty and suffering, Stevie now realizes, are results of the injustice of poverty. Conrad often has a character in a novel 'sum-up' in an apparently simple statement a theme which Conrad then develops in a complex way. This is the case with the insight Stevie now expresses after great effort:

Charity cottages like those to which Winnie's mother consigns herself, which 'might have been devised in kindness as a place of training for the still more straitened circumstances of the grave'. (The Secret Agent).

> It was as if he was trying to fit all the words he could remember to his sentiments in order to get some sort of corresponding idea. And, as a matter of fact, he got it at last. He hung back to utter it at once.
> 'Bad world for poor people.'

The fates of Verloc, Winnie and Stevie are sometimes described as 'tragic'. But in *The Secret Agent* Conrad seems

to be trying for a new literary style, which is neither comic nor tragic but a disorientating mixture of the two. The final image of Mr Verloc's body, as seen by Ossipon, is both farcical and sinister at the same time:

> But the true sense of the scene he was beholding came to Ossipon through the contemplation of the hat. It seemed an extraordinary thing, an ominous object, a sign. Black, and rim upward, it lay on the floor before the couch as if prepared to receive the contributions of pence from people who would come presently to behold Mr Verloc in the fullness of his domestic ease reposing on a sofa.

The image of the hat waiting for coins offers the reader an image of a dead body – and Conrad's own novel? – as if it were a comic turn. The way the novel itself has shown us the truth behind Mr Verloc's 'domestic ease' has also been oddly funny and also sinister. In 'Heart of Darkness' Marlow complains that his experience is like a dream and that it is impossible to find a language to 'convey the dream-sensation, that commingling of absurdity, surprise and bewilderment which is the very essence of dreams'. In this extraordinary last image of Verloc Conrad has achieved the 'commingling' of these incongrous elements in a new style, not open to the old definitions of comedy and tragedy. The great German novelist Thomas Mann, discussing *The Secret Agent*, precisely expressed this new quality that Conrad has brought to the novel:

> The gaze turned upon the horrible is clear, lively, dry-eyed, almost gratified; the spirit of the narration is impressively English, and at the same time it is ultra-modern, post-middle-class. For I feel that, broadly and essentially, the striking feature of modern art is that it has ceased to recognize the categories of tragic and comic, or the dramatic classifications, tragedy and comedy. It sees life as tragi-comedy with the result that the grotesque is its most genuine style – to the extent, indeed, that today that is the only guise in which the sublime may appear.

One more layer is added to the novel's absurd incongruities by the fact that this 'ultra-modern' and 'post-middle-class' work was first published in a magazine whose title makes it sound anything but: *Ridgway's. A Militant Weekly for God and Country.*

Opposite *Thomas Mann, the German novelist who recognized Conrad's talent.*

4

'Heart of
Darkness'

Conrad's manuscript
of 'Heart of
Darkness'. 'Oh! The
horror!'

Conrad's agonizing Congo experiences of 1890 were re-worked nine years later into 'Heart of Darkness', which is generally regarded as one of the greatest short novels in the English language. It is a crucial work in the development of modern literature, in that it establishes the dominant theme of twentieth-century writing: fear and disillusion about Western man's place in the world and the values by which he lives. The narrator and central character Marlow travels up the Congo to meet the demonic trader Kurtz. He witnesses the violence and hypocrisy of his colonizing culture and his faith in the Western world and even his own sanity is threatened. T.S. Eliot indicated how influential he felt the novel to be when he used the paragraph ending in Kurtz's famous summing-up, 'The horror! The horror!' as the epigraph to his great poem *The Waste Land* (1922). The degeneration of the trader, to whom all Europe contributed, stands for Eliot as a model of modern man in a world the poet sees, in a phrase that recalls the trenches of World War One and the bone-strewn Congo of 'Heart of Darkness', as a 'rat's alley / Where the dead men lost their bones'.

While working in the Congo as a steamboat captain for the Belgian trading company Anonyme Belge Conrad kept a short *Congo Diary*, which mixes useful technical information with abruptly jotted accounts of events he witnessed. The final entry gives some impression of the horrors he saw but gives very little idea of his feelings:

Friday 1st August, 1890
  Row between the carriers and a man stating himself in Gov[ernment] employ, about a mat. Blows with sticks raining hard. Stopped it. Chief came with a youth about 13 suffering from gunshot wound in the head. Bullet entered about an inch above the right eyebrow and came out a little inside. The roots of the hair fairly parted in the middle of the brow in a line with the bridge of the nose. Bone not damaged apparently. Gave him a little glycerine to put on the wound made by the bullet on coming out. Haron not very well. Mosquitoes. Frogs. Beastly. Glad to see the end of this stupid tramp. Feel rather seedy. Sun rose red. Very hot day. Wind S[ou]th.
  General direction of march – NE by N
  Distance – about 17 miles

This could be seen as the most disturbing – because least

A placid image of Congo colonization for Western consumption from Countries of the World, *late 1870s. The colony had been opened up by Stanley's exploration of 1876–7.*

disturbed – passage Conrad ever wrote. He unreflectively notes his own humane actions in stopping the carriers being beaten and dressing the boy's wound, but the horrors of a racial violence seemingly both routine and arbitrary are not allowed to disturb the briskly matter-of-fact style. The limp term 'Beastly' is used to describe not this violence but the irritations of frogs and mosquitoes. The entry ends in business-like fashion with technical information for future reference. It is as if Conrad threw himself into his work in order not to reflect too deeply on what he was doing. Only years later in 'Heart of Darkness' was he finally able to examine his feelings. The distance between the off-hand style of the diary and the imaginative intensity of 'Heart of Darkness' can be seen from the following description of a grove filled with Africans who have been worked nearly to death:

> Near the same tree two or more bundles of acute angles sat with their legs drawn up. One, with his chin propped on his knees stared at nothing, in an intolerable and appalling manner: his brother phantom rested its forehead, as if overcome by a great weariness; and all about others were scattered in every pose of contorted collapse, as if some picture of a massacre or a pestilence. While I stood horror-struck, one of these creatures rose to his hands and knees, and went off on all-fours towards the river to drink. He lapped out of his hand, then sat up in the sunlight, crossing his shins in front of him, and after a time let his woolly head fall on his breastbone.

Opposite *Conrad in 1903, shortly after he had written 'Heart of Darkness'.*

'In the opinon of the State the soldiers, in killing game for food, wasted the State cartridges, and in consequence the soldiers, to show their officers that they did not expend the cartridges extravagantly...for each empty cartridge brought in a human hand.' A photograph from Roger Casement's report.

Opposite 'The word "ivory" rang in the air. You would think they were praying to it'.

Though some significant touches remain, indicating a marked sense of distance from what he sees – 'as if some picture', 'I stood horror-struck' – the total effect is such as to justify Marlow's insistence that his stories should arouse both 'compassion' and 'indignation'. In the *Congo Diary* Conrad refuses to let the atrocities he witnesses unsettle his attention to his duties. In 'Heart of Darkness' Conrad creates a character who embodies just such an attitude. The passage continues with the appearance of the company accountant, a meticulously dressed man with oiled hair and a parasol who 'keeps his books in apple-pie order'. Marlow finds himself admiring this sinisterly comic figure and his starchy fussiness over profits and appearances, ' . . . in the great demoralization of the land he kept up his appearance. That's backbone. His starched collars and got-up shirt fronts were achievements of character.' The incident is brilliantly provocative. Is the keeping up of appearances to be despised or admired?

Opposite '...a stream of manufactured goods, rubbishy cottons, beads, and brass-wire sent into the depths of darkness, and in return came a precious trickle of ivory.' ('Heart of Darkness').

What would be a genuine 'achievement of character' in such a situation? Are Western values no more than a 'got-up shirt-front'? Conrad's 'answers' to such questions are never clear-cut. As readers we need to be aware how much, if he does attempt to answer them, the responses come in terms of clear 'eloquence' – a dubious term in this novel given that Kurtz is famous for it. Rather Conrad's method involves a subtle use of imagery 'difficult and evanescent'. In this passage Conrad uses a dense patterning of images whereby key words take on various meanings from their reappearances in contrasting contexts. So Marlow's admiration for the accountant's 'backbone' rings peculiarly hollow in a novel so concerned with bones, skulls, skeletons, and the 'back-breaking' business of trading in that other type of bone, ivory. With particular malignancy the term echoes the last word of two paragraphs before – the dying African's protruding 'breastbone'.

The accountant is a fine example of Conrad's ability to combine the most realistic detail with a larger, symbolic meaning. The black American, George Washington Williams, who protested in a letter of 1890 to Leopold II of Belgium about 'the deceit, fraud, robberies, arson, murder,

King Leopold II of Belgium.

slave-raiding, and general policy of cruelty' of his regime in the Congo, also points out the absurd obsessiveness of Belgian bureaucracy whereby if an agent buys two eggs he has to record the act in nine separate entries. In depicting the combination of meticulous bureaucracy with atrocity Conrad anticipates a peculiar feature of twentieth-century history. He makes of the Congo accountant as telling an image of modern man as the insipid Verloc and the demonic Kurtz.

The novel begins with the anonymous narrator sitting with Marlow on board the yawl *Nellie* waiting for the River Thames' tide to turn. He muses nostalgically upon 'the great-Knight errants of the sea' who in Tudor times set out on that very tide on their glorious voyages of exploration and conquest bearing 'the germs of empires'. His romantic nationalism recalls that of the narrator of *The Nigger of the 'Narcissus'* and also that of Conrad's more popular contemporary novelist, Kipling, who called Britain's colonial agents 'the new knighthood'. But germs can, of course, be the sort that are spread rather than sown and Marlow chips in to offer his own image of national history. He completely reverses what Conrad, with sly irony, had had the initial narrator call the 'gigantic tale' of British supremacy. He imagines the original Roman invaders feeling the 'utter savagery' of barbaric Britain close around them.

In this sceptical and questioning vein Marlow's story of imperialism and savagery in the Congo begins. In 1898 the explorer Henry Morton Stanley praised the Belgian regime in the Congo:

Carlyle says that 'to subdue mutiny, discord, widespread despair by manfulness, justice, mercy, to let light on chaos, and make it instead a green flowery world, is beyond other greatness, work for a God!' Who can doubt that God chose the King for His instrument to redeem this vast slave park . . . King Leopold found the Congo . . . cursed by cannibalism, savagery, and despair; and he has been trying with a patience, which I can never sufficiently admire, to relieve it of its horrors, rescue it from its oppressors, and save it from perdition.

Conrad realizes that the impressive terms that for Stanley bear straightforward meanings are capable of being twisted in the most deceitful and nightmarish ways. 'Heart

Opposite *Explorer and popular Victorian hero, Henry Morton Stanley. His enthusiastic memoir,* The Congo and the Founding of its Free State; A Story of Work and Exploration *is ironically echoed in 'Heart of Darkness'. The meeting of Marlow and Kurtz is influenced by Stanley's famous discovery of Livingstone.*

of Darkness' explores the unstable meanings of those potent words used to justify colonialism: manfulness, light, savagery, despair and horror. In dramatizing how the demonic trader Kurtz writes and speaks with inspiring 'eloquence' and yet performs rites of 'unspeakable' savagery, Conrad highlights how Western civilization's high-sounding language has become frighteningly detached from the actual nature of its actions.

As a boy Marlow had a passion for maps and a particular ambition to investigate 'the blank space of delightful mystery' indicating Central Africa, which was gradually being filled in with names and features as it was explored and colonized. Years later as a young seaman an opportunity arises to fulfil his ambition when the skipper of a river steamboat carrying ivory in the Belgian Congo is killed. Marlow travels to the colonial company's headquarters in a city he describes as 'a whited sepulchre', a biblical image for hypocrisy, as Conrad had travelled to Brussels in 1890. In the company's offices he encounters two ominous women knitting black wool and a doctor who asks to measure his skull because of his interest in 'the mental changes of individuals' whom the company sends into the Congo. The combination of the mysterious women and the keen doctor neatly shows how Conrad blends the traditional and the modern. They also suggest different ways of looking at the novel. The knitting women recall the Fates of classical mythology who spin and cut the thread of people's lives. They are one of the novel's range of references to mythology and classic works of Western literature.

Another such reference is developed as Marlow's journey through the successive 'Company', 'Central' and 'Inner' stations echoes the stages of the journey into the inner circle of hell taken by Virgil and Dante in the latter's medieval religious poem *The Divine Comedy*. These elements of the novel suggest that it should be read as we read a myth; as a statement on the timeless problems of the 'human condition'. In contrast, the doctor who admits to being something of an 'alienist', or psychiatrist, with his interest in insanity and analysing 'the mental changes of individuals', is very much a product of Conrad's own period when the sciences of psychology and psychiatry were first being developed. The novel itself has a modern interest in tracing 'mental changes' in its characters. And

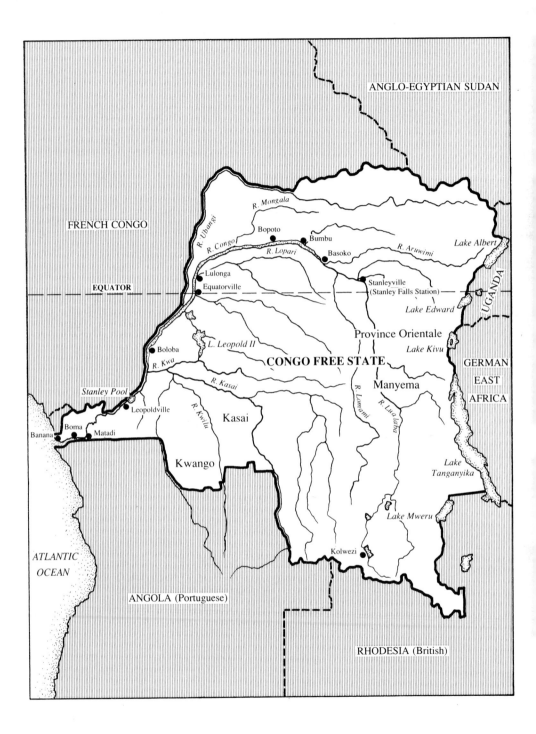

Opposite *Central Africa in the 1880s was divided between Western colonial powers. The ironically entitled 'Congo Free State' is labelled with features bearing the names of Stanley and King Leopold of Belgium and was more than seventy times larger than Leopold's own Belgian kingdom.*

Left *Dante and Virgil in Hell. An illustration by Gustave Doré for Dante's* The Divine Comedy. *Marlow's account of his Congo experience is haunted by echoes of Dante's poem. '...it seemed to me I had stepped into the gloomy circle of some Inferno.'*

rather than being as timeless as a myth, it carefully evokes the psychological pressures characteristic of life in the West in the late nineteenth century, which Conrad suggests is itself like a massive trading and colonizing company.

For Marlow the journey up the Congo becomes a pilgrimage to meet Kurtz, the man of reputedly brilliant talent and eloquence who sends down more ivory than all the company's other traders put together. Conrad's imagination is at its most vivid when he describes Marlow's observations on his journey. Colonialism's brutal futility is memorably captured in image after image;

a natural ravine is clogged with a 'wanton smash-up' of imported drainage pipes; a 'native' fearfully tends the ship's boiler thinking he serves the thirsty devil he has been told inhabits it; the grass grows through the ribs of a trader's corpse in a village abandoned in panic upon his accidental killing, colonialist and local community destroyed equally by their encounter.

In *The Nigger of the 'Narcissus'* Conrad had suggested that the ship's voyage had been tinged with unreality. Describing how 'the moonlight clung to her like a frosted mist' the narrator comments that 'nothing in her was real, nothing was distinct and solid but the heavy shadows that filled her decks with their unceasing stir'. In 'Heart of Darkness' this unreality becomes the basic condition of Marlow's experience. Conrad expands the image of the shadowy journey to suggest an eerie venture beyond the bounds of reality, where one's senses seem useless, the physical world loses its solidity and one is strangely alone.

Opposite *"You should have heard him say, 'My ivory'...'My Intended, my ivory, my station, my river, my —' everything belonged to him."* ('Heart of Darkness'). A white trader overseeing ivory collection, in 1892.

> What we could see was just the steamer we were on, her outlines blurred as though she had been on the point of dissolving, and a misty strip of water, perhaps two feet broad, around her – and that was all. The rest of the world was nowhere as far as our eyes and ears were concerned. Just nowhere. Gone, disappeared; swept off without leaving a whisper or a shadow behind.

The experience throws Marlow's sense of reality into confusion. As he puts it; 'For a while I would feel that I belonged to a world of straight-forward facts; but the feeling would not last long. Something would turn up to scare it away.' For Marlow the suspicious term 'reality' takes on a variety of meanings. He resists dwelling on the significance of his experience by repairing the 'biscuit-tin' steamboat, claiming that absorption in such activity can create 'your own reality – for yourself, not for others – what no man can ever know'. And yet at other moments he realizes that such 'reality' amounts to no more than keeping tin-pot illusions afloat whilst ignoring 'inner truth':

> When you have to attend to things of that sort, to the things of the surface, the reality – the reality I tell you – fades. The inner truth is hidden – luckily, luckily. But I felt it all the same.

Marlow experiences a feeling central to the literature of modernism: the experience of contemporary history, 'that vast panorama of anarchy and futility,' as T. S. Eliot called it, is so shocking and incomprehensible as to challenge all familiar concepts of truth and meaning. Marlow senses that the truths of the nineteenth-century Western world, whose products include its colonialism and sense of racial superiority, are merely Western man's 'own reality – for himself, not for others'.

Kurtz too, it would appear, has set up his own 'reality'. His extraordinary trading success is gradually explained as it emerges that in the inaccessible Inner Station he has made himself the centre of a savage cult. The encampment where he indulges in 'unspeakable rites' is ringed with heads on posts. Conrad's great theme had always been the individual's struggle for self-possession. The colonial

Opposite *Sigmund Freud, pioneer of psychoanalysis. Freud's analysis of the unconscious mind is contemporary with and similar to Conrad's interest in his characters' dreams and deliriums.*

Conrad's manuscript of 'Heart of Darkness', showing the famous line, 'Mistah Kurtz – he dead.' T. S. Eliot used this line as the epigraph to his poem 'The Hollow Men' (1925).

exploitation he depicts here is a sordid scramble for possession pure and simple, a 'robbery with violence' that destroys the self. In one sense Kurtz is the embodiment of the sheer obsession with owning that fuels the colonial venture:

> You should have heard him say 'My ivory' . . . 'My Intended, my ivory, my station, my river, my —' . . . everything belonged to him – but that was a trifle. The thing was to know what he belonged to, how many powers of darkness claimed him for their own.

The last sentence indicates what Conrad is continually suggesting but never directly states – the repulsive 'powers of darkness' to which Kurtz belongs are those of his own culture. 'All Europe contributed to the making of Kurtz.' London too, as Marlow's first words put it, 'has been one of the dark places of the earth'. Weakened with unspecified excesses that may include cannibalism, Kurtz dies having 'summed up' with the words 'The horror! The horror!' The horror of a colonialism he has helped to create has utterly reversed the meanings expressed by Marlow's aunt of the West's mission in Africa as 'weaning those ignorant millions from their horrid ways'. With a typically Conradian ironic detail this 'supreme moment of complete knowledge', as Marlow interprets it, occurs when Kurtz, like the delirious Jimmy before him, believes he is in the dark when the light is actually burning 'within a foot of his eyes'.

Returning to the sepulchural city Marlow visits Kurtz's 'Intended', or fiancée, who retains her image of him as an inspired man of genius and begs to hear his last words. His actual words seem to swell in the air but Marlow cannot bring himself to reveal them and he answers 'your name'. Conrad has pointedly avoided giving the Intended a name, which leaves open the possibility that this famous lie has an element of truth in it. The Intended represents the delicate sensibilities of those who want to be protected from reality. She embodies the 'great and saving illusion' of Western ignorance, and so is, in a sense, merely a tragically dignified version of the accountant's obsession with 'keeping up appearances'. In this sense her delicacy is a source of lies and horror. In *Lord Jim* Marlow meditates upon 'the essential sincerity of falsehood'.

Opposite *Rudyard Kipling, colonial enthusiast and novelist whose sales greatly outstripped Conrad's.*

94

Propaganda for British colonialism from The British Workman, *1859. Queen Victoria recommends the Bible to a native ambassador, 'This is the secret of England's greatness'.*

A comparison with Kipling will highlight how fundamentally 'Heart of Darkness' breaks with traditional imperialist themes. Kipling's short story 'Thrown Away' (1888) describes how a naïve English officer fresh from his Sandhurst training is posted to India, loses heavily in gambling and, oppressed by 'disgrace', commits suicide. He is found by a major and another officer who narrates the story, who agree to destroy the anguished letters he had written home. Concluding that the truth would be a 'Nice sort of thing to spring on an English family' they concoct a 'big, written lie . . . it was no time for little lies you understand' – that he had died of cholera. The mother writes to the major of her 'obligation' to him and the narrator concludes 'all things considered, she was under an obligation, but not exactly as she meant.'

Kipling's story shares with Conrad's the concerns of a late Victorian and Edwardian England in governing a declining and morally dubious empire; most particularly the crises of guilt and disillusion that can drive someone to 'the end of the tether' in an alien 'outpost of progress' and the question of how much truth, if any, to tell those back home. But their handling of these issues is crucially different. Kipling avoids probing the boy's evidently disturbed psychology and so avoids the question of the mental pressures of the colonizer's role. In an emphatic opening statement the narrator blames the parents for bringing him up 'too soft'. That such questions are of central interest to Marlow is evident from his first words when he vividly pictures the anxieties of a 'decent young man in a toga' colonizing ancient Britain, who feels the 'utter savagery . . . close around him. Imagine the growing regrets, the longing to escape, the powerless disgust, the surrender, the hate'.

Kipling appears to agree with his characters' attitude that appearances must be kept up even at the expense of a 'big lie'. (The term recalls the initial narrator's 'gigantic tale'.) When the major asks the soldier/narrator if he would lie about the boy he smartly replies 'It's my profession'. This is as much as the story says on the matter and perhaps disturbingly expresses something of Kipling's attitude to his own role as the popular storyteller of colonialism. (With deep irony of which perhaps he was not conscious this story of 'big lies' from abroad appeared in a volume entitled *Plain Tales from the Hills*.) Marlow, by contrast, is guilt-ridden at his decision that the truth would be 'too dark altogether' to tell the Intended, which accounts for his otherwise inexplicable early outburst, 'You know I hate detest and can't bear a lie. There is a taint of death . . . in lies – which is exactly what I hate and detest in the world'. In the parlour of the Intended, where the elegant furnishings of bourgeois life appear as funeral trappings – the monumental fireplace is like a tomb, the grand piano, with ivory keys, no doubt, gleams darkly 'like a sombre and polished sarcophagus' – we question, like Marlow, whether such death-saturated life is worth lying for.

5

Conclusion

A glance at the chronology of Conrad's life will show that his writing career spanned a period of massive historical and artistic change in Europe. His writing can be seen to chart these changes and his work is thus a bridge between Victorian and modern fiction. The Victorian qualities of his work include his emphasis on the weighty moral choices his characters have to make and a marked respect for the values of work and duty. But his view of contemporary history and his presentation of character have the specifically modern qualities that make his work a crucial influence on the literature of modernism.

Conrad's major characters are clearly creations of the age of the founder of psychoanalysis, Sigmund Freud, with whom Conrad shares a fascination for the powerful hidden qualities of the human mind. Conrad's interest in disturbed psychological states such as Jimmy's delirium, Stevie's creation of his chaotic 'art' and Marlow's traumatic experiences in the Congo, show an awareness like Freud's of how much vital activity in the mind goes on beneath the level of our everyday experiences and emotions. They also express an attitude that becomes a key feature of twentieth-century art: a questioning view of what is normally regarded as sanity and reality.

Conrad's bleak view of the values of his culture and the dehumanizing progress of technology and colonialism also makes his view of contemporary history one that greatly influences twentieth-century writing. James Joyce in his great modernist novel *Ulysses* (1922) has his character Stephen call history 'a nightmare from which I am trying to awake'. It is a nightmare which in Marlow's Congo experience Conrad had bravely explored more than twenty years earlier.

But it is wrong to suggest that Conrad's work leaves us only a feeling of pessimism and disillusion. In a letter to the *New York Times* Conrad again stressed his characteristic view of life as made up of contradictions, but concluded that it is a condition that can be inspiring as well as disturbing:

> The only basis of creative work lies in the courageous recognition of all the irreconcilable antagonisms that make our life so enigmatic, so burdensome, so fascinating, so dangerous – so full of hope.

Conrad in 1923, the year before his death, at the time of his exhausting reading tour of the USA.

Glossary

Agent provacateur A person employed to detect suspected spies, etc. by tempting them to come out into the open.

Anarchism A political doctrine that states that all governments should be abolished. Out of the ensuing chaos anarchists believe a natural order would be formed.

Autobiography The story of one's life written by oneself.

Breaking strain The strain or effort necessary to exert on an object to break it.

Colonialism A policy whereby one nation sends settlers to, and then rules, another nation as part of its empire. Also known as 'imperialism'.

Dissident A person who disagrees with an established government, etc.

Evanescent Fading, disappearing quickly.

Imperialism *see* 'colonialism'.

Interiorization A style of narration which gives the reader insight into the movements of a character's mind.

Latitude A line parallel to the equator used, with a line of longitude, to chart a particular position on the globe.

Martial law When normal law is suspended and an army takes over the role of government.

Melodrama A sensational dramatic piece with crude appeals to emotions and, usually, a happy ending.

Merchant service Shipping employed in commerce and trade.

Metaphor Application of the name of a descriptive term or phrase to an object to which it is not literally applicable

Modernism A movement in the arts that flourished in the decade after the First World War (1914-18). In literature writers such as James Joyce, Virginia Woolf and T.S. Eliot experimented with a shifting variety of styles to express the sense of disillusion and fragmentation they saw as characteristic of contemporary life.

Omniscient Literally, 'all-knowing'. Used to describe the narration characteristic of nineteenth-century fiction, such as George Eliot's, in which a narrator gives an authoritative account and explanation of all aspects of the story.

Petit bourgeois Middle class, humdrum, conventional.

Reactionary Taking a hard-line political view opposed to change.

Red Ensign The flag of the British Merchant Navy.

Retrospect A survey of past time or events.

Surrealism A twentieth-century movement in art and literature aiming to express the subconscious mind and to represent and interpret dreams.

Yawl A type of sailing boat.

List of Dates

Conrad's Life	Other artistic and historical events
1857 Conrad born in Berdyczow in Russian Poland.	The Indian Mutiny. Flaubert's *Madame Bovary*.
1861 His father Apollo Korzeniowski arrested for anti-Russian activity.	Dicken's *Great Expectations*.
1862 Apollo and wife Eva sent into Russian exile with Conrad.	
1865 Eva dies of tuberculosis.	Rudyard Kipling born.
1869 Apollo dies. Conrad adopted by his uncle Tadeusz.	Tolstoy's *War and Peace*.
1874 Leaves Poland for Marseilles to start sea career.	First Impressionist exhibition, Paris.
1878 Suicide attempt. Later joins British Merchant Navy.	Congress of Berlin.
1880 Qualifies as second mate.	George Eliot dies.
1883 Shipwrecked.	Marx dies. Mussolini born.
1884 Qualifies as first mate.	
1886 Becomes a British subject. Qualifies as master.	Hardy's *The Mayor of Casterbridge*.
1888 First command on *Otago*.	T.S. Eliot born.

1889	Resigns from *Otago* and begins *Almayer's Folly*.	Hitler born.
1890	Works as steamer captain in the Belgian Congo.	Ibsen's *Hedda Gabler*.
1894	*Almayer's Folly* accepted by Unwin's reader, Edward Garnett.	Dreyfus Affair begins in France. Greenwich bomb outrage.
1895	*Almayer's Folly*.	Engels dies. Hardy's *Jude the Obscure*. Crane's *The Red Badge of Courage*.
1896	Marries Jessie George. *An Outcast of the Islands* published.	McKinley becomes President.
1897	*The Nigger of the 'Narcissus'*.	Queen Victoria's Diamond Jubilee.
1898	*Tales of Unrest*. Birth of son Boris.	Spanish-American War. Wells's *The War of the Worlds*.
1899	'Heart of Darkness' serialized in *Blackwood's Magazine*.	1899-1902 Boer War.
1900	*Lord Jim*.	Freud's *The Interpretation of Dreams*.
1901	*The Inheritors*, a collaboration with Ford Madox Ford.	Queen Victoria dies, succeeded by Edward VII.
1902	*Youth*, including 'Heart of Darkness'.	Chekov's *The Three Sisters*.
1904	*Nostromo*.	Russo-Japanese War. Henry James's *The Golden Bowl*.
1906	*The Mirror of the Sea*. Second son John born.	Massive electoral victory for the Liberal Party. John Galsworthy's *The Man of Property*. Samuel Beckett born.

1907	*The Secret Agent.*	Strindberg's *Ghost Sonata.* Picasso's *Les Demoiselles*
1910	'The Secret Sharer'. Conrad has a breakdown on completing *Under Western Eyes.*	*d' Avignon.* Freud's work begins to be widely known.
1911	*Under Western Eyes.*	Suffragette agitation increases.
1912	*Some Reminiscences,* later called *A Personal Record. Twixt Land and Sea.*	
1913	*Chance.*	D.H. Lawrence's *Sons and Lovers.* Proust's *Swann's Way.*
1914	*Chance* becomes a bestseller.	1914-18 First World War. Joyce's *Dubliners.*
1915	*Within the Tides. Victory.*	Zeppelin attacks begin on London.
1917	*The Shadow Line.*	Russian Revolution. T.S. Eliot's *Prufrock and Other Observations.*
1919	*The Arrow of Gold.*	Treaty of Versailles.
1920	*The Rescue.*	Poles repel Russian invasion. D.H. Lawrence's *Women in Love.*
1921	*Notes on Life and Letters.*	Charlie Chaplin's first feature film *The Kid.*
1922	Play of *The Secret Agent* a flop.	Mussolini, Europe's first fascist dictator, comes to power in Italy. T.S. Eliot's *The*
1923	*The Rover.* Successful, but exhausting reading tour of USA.	*Waste Land.* Joyce's *Ulysses.*
1924	Turns down a knighthood. Dies in August. Buried at Canterbury.	Ramsey MacDonald heads Britain's first Labour Government. Lenin dies.

Further Reading

Conrad's diaries and autobiographical writings
NAJDER, Z. (ed.) *Congo Diary and other uncollected Pieces* (Doubleday and Co., New York, 1978)
The Mirror of the Sea and *A Personal record* (Oxford University Press, World's Classics, 1988)

Conrad's fiction
All Conrad's completed novels are published by Penguin books including those discussed here:
'Heart of Darkness' (Penguin Modern Classics, 1973)
The Nigger of the 'Narcissus' (Penguin Classics, 1988)
The Secret Agent (Penguin Modern Classics, 1963)
'The Secret Sharer' in *'Twixt Land and Sea* (Penguin Classics, 1988)
The Shadow Line (Penguin Classics, 1986)

Biography, history and criticism
BAINES, JOCELYN, *Joseph Conrad* (Penguin, London, 1971)
GILLON, ADAM, *Joseph Conrad* (Twaynes' English Authors Series, Boston, 1982)
HUNTER, JEFFERSON, *Edwardian Fiction* (Cambridge, Mass., 1982)
HOBSBAWM, E.J., *The Age of Empire 1875 – 1914* (London, 1987)
PAGE, NORMAN, *A Conrad Companion* (London, 1986)
TENNANT, ROGER, *Joseph Conrad: A Biography* (London, 1981)
WATTS, CEDRIC, *A Preface to Conrad* (New York, 1982)
WOOLF, VIRGINIA, *Collected Essays* Volume 2 (London, 1966)

Picture acknowledgements

The author and publishers would like to thank the following for allowing their illustrations to be reproduced in this book: The Manuscript Department, William R. Perkins Library, Duke University 7, 10, 12, 28, 30, 31 (both), 35, 37, 79, 99; Mary Evans Picture Library 8, 13, 17, 20, 22, 23, 27, 34, 42, 43, 50, 51, 52, 53, 55, 56–7, 58, 60, 61, 62, 63, 64, 66, 69, 72, 73, 74, 78, 81, 85, 90, 92, 95, 96; Hulton Picture Company 11, 39, 40, 59, 65; The Billie Love Collection 41, 46, 48–9, 54; The Mansell Collection 14, 15, 16, 24, 45, 68, 82, 83; The National Film Archive 19; The National Maritime Museum 18, 21, 25, 36; Topham 26, 44, 71, 80; Yale University Library 76, 93. The maps on pages 87 and 88 were drawn by Peter Bull. All other pictures are from the Wayland Picture Library.

Index